HOLIDAYS

HOLIDAYS

50 Recipes from the
Chicago Tribune

TRIBUNE
PUBLISHING

ORLANDO / 1993

CHICAGO TRIBUNE

Carol Haddix: Food Guide Editor
JeanMarie Brownson: Assistant
  Food Guide Editor
and the food staff of the *Chicago Tribune*

Cover photograph by Bill Hogan

Inside and back cover photographs by
Tony Berardi, John Dziekan, Bob Fila,
Sally Good, Bill Hogan, David Klobucar

Design by Bill Henderson,
Tribune Publishing

Copyright © 1993
Tribune Publishing
75 East Amelia Street
Orlando, Florida 32801

Printed in the United States

FIRST EDITION

TRIBUNE PUBLISHING

Editorial Director: George C. Biggers III
Managing Editor: Dixie Kasper
Senior Editor: Kathleen M. Kiely
Production Editor: Ken Paskman
Designers: Bill Henderson
       Eileen Schechner
       Joy Dickinson

For information:
Tribune Publishing
P.O. Box 1100
Orlando, Florida 32802

This cookbook series would not be possible
without the help of those who produce
the weekly *Chicago Tribune Food Guide*.

Thanks especially go to
Connie Coning, Pat Dailey, Steven Pratt and William Rice.

Appreciation for art and photography help go to
Tony Berardi, Charles Cherney, John Dziekan,
Kevin Fewell, Bob Fila, Tom Heinz,
Bill Hogan and David Klobucar.

Thanks to Dianne Hugh and Patti Florez
for food styling and to Cheryl Barcal for photo styling.

Kudos for research help go to Karen Blair.

And thanks to editors Brenda Butler, Howard Tyner,
Joe Leonard and Jack Fuller.

— Carol Haddix
JeanMarie Brownson

CONTENTS

Introduction

ix

Index

100

Family, friends and food. The three often go hand in hand whenever a holiday rolls around. Festivities require special dishes. Cooks want to please guests with food that tastes great, looks great and shows the care and love that went into it.

While old favorite recipes make up the bulk of holiday foods (who can imagine a Thanksgiving without turkey and Grandma's stuffing?), there often comes the time to try something new, something not handed down for generations.

When that time comes, we hope you will turn to the 50 recipes here, all tested in the *Chicago Tribune* kitchen and presented in the newspaper's food section. We like to think that our readers have adopted some of these dishes as their new holiday "traditions."

We have included suggested menus with each holiday (with selected recipes highlighted in bold type), but they really are only a guide. Feel free to mix and match particular dishes from one holiday to the next. And, knowing that holiday cooking often can be the most stressful, we have included information on preparing parts of dishes ahead of the holiday. Hopefully that will ease the time spent in the kitchen on a special day when you would rather mingle with friends and family. After all, that's what holidays are for!

LIGHT PARTY HERB DIP

Whether you've made a low-fat resolution or not, this dip is a sensational way to snack without guilt. The choice of herbs can be varied. Fresh basil, cilantro and tarragon are other good choices. Serve the dip with a selection of raw vegetables. If diet is no object on New Year's Day, pull out all the stops with these fresh homemade whiskey sours.

Preparation time: 10 minutes
Yield: About 3 cups

2 cups low-fat cottage cheese

$^2/_3$ cup chopped fresh parsley

$^1/_2$ cup chopped fresh dill

$^1/_4$ cup each: fresh lemon juice, olive oil

2 tablespoons Dijon-style mustard

4 teaspoons capers, drained

Put all ingredients into food processor or electric blender. Process until smooth. Serve with assorted raw vegetables, crackers or slices of French bread.

AUNT DOROTHY'S WHISKEY SOURS

$2^2/_3$ cups bourbon

$^3/_4$ cup fresh lemon juice

$^1/_2$ cup superfine sugar

24 ice cubes, plus optional cubes for the glasses

MIDNIGHT SUPPER FOR EIGHT

Light party herb dip

Whiskey sours or Champagne

Crudites and crackers

Corn blinis with cured salmon

Shrimp in coconut curry sauce

Endive and apple salad with blue cheese and walnuts

Bread sticks

Assorted cookies and fruit sorbets

8 thin slices lemon

8 maraschino cherries

Preparation time: 15 minutes
Yield: 8 servings

1. Pour bourbon into a large pitcher. Add lemon juice and sugar. Stir vigorously.

2. Just before serving, add ice cubes to the pitcher and stir until the liquid is well chilled.

3. If desired, place additional ice cubes in 8 rocks glasses. Divide the batch of sours among the glasses. Garnish each glass with a lemon slice and cherry; serve.

ENDIVE AND APPLE SALAD WITH BLUE CHEESE AND WALNUTS

This partnership is classic, with each ingredient contributing to the final harmony. The slightly bitter flavor of endive is offset by tart apples, tangy cheese and toasted walnuts. Developed for a feature on apples, it was named one of the Food Guide's Best of the Year recipes in 1991.

Preparation time: 25 minutes
Yield: 8 servings

DRESSING

6 tablespoons olive oil

1/4 cup each: red wine vinegar, crumbled blue cheese

2 tablespoons each: walnut oil, minced parsley

4 teaspoons grainy mustard

Salt, freshly ground black pepper

SALAD

2 McIntosh apples

6 heads Belgian endive

2 large ribs celery

1/2 cup each: minced toasted walnuts (see note), crumbled blue cheese

1. For dressing, put all ingredients into food processor or blender; mix until smooth.

2. For salad, cut apples in half lengthwise and remove core. Cut unpeeled apple into matchstick strips. Reserve several large endive spears for garnish and cut the rest into strips. Cut celery into strips.

3. Mix apples, endive and celery; toss with dressing. Divide among salad plates; sprinkle walnuts and cheese over top. Garnish with endive spears.

Note: To toast walnuts, spread walnuts in a baking pan. Toast in a 350-degree oven until golden and aromatic, 8 to 10 minutes. Watch carefully so nuts do not burn. Immediately transfer to a plate to cool.

CORN BLINIS WITH CURED SALMON

Joachim Splichal, chef at Patina Restaurant in Los Angeles, designed these miniature corn pancakes for a benefit brunch held in Chicago. A luxurious splurge, they're easily made and quite elegant for any festive holiday celebration.

Preparation time: 35 minutes
Standing time: 30 minutes
Cooking time: 20 minutes
Yield: 24 blinis

BLINIS

3 ears fresh corn or 1 cup frozen corn kernels

6 tablespoons butter, clarified (see note)

1 medium shallot, finely chopped

$^1/_3$ cup whipping cream

2 large eggs

1 cup all-purpose flour

$^1/_3$ cup milk

2 tablespoons chopped fresh parsley

FILLING

6 ounces thinly sliced cured salmon (gravlax) or smoked fish such as salmon, sturgeon, whitefish or eel

GARNISH

3 tablespoons sour cream

$^1/_2$ each: red and yellow bell pepper, roasted, peeled, diced (see note)

$^1/_4$ cup chopped fresh chives

1. Heat pan of water to boil. Cut corn kernels from the cob; add to water. Cook 2 minutes. Drain and set aside.

2. Heat 1 tablespoon of the butter in a large skillet. Add shallot and corn; cook and stir 2 minutes. Add cream; simmer until reduced and slightly thickened, about 3 minutes.

3. Put eggs and flour into a blender. Add milk; blend for 1 minute. Heat 1 generous tablespoon of the butter in a small pan until it begins to brown. Add browned butter to blender; blend until a batter forms.

4. Combine batter and corn mixture in large bowl. Refrigerate for 30 minutes. Just before cooking, stir in parsley.

5. Heat a large skillet or griddle. Add enough of the remaining butter to coat the surface; drop 1 table-spoonful of batter at intervals into the pan for each blini. Cook until golden, about 1 minute; turn and cook the second side until cooked through, about 30 seconds. Remove to a plate set in a warm oven. Repeat, adding butter to pan as needed, until all the batter has been used.

6. To serve, sandwich two warm blinis with a slice of salmon. Garnish the top with a dab of sour cream, diced bell pepper and chives.

Note: To clarify butter, melt butter in small saucepan or in bowl in micro-wave oven. Use a spoon to remove white foam from surface. Slowly pour only the clear yellow liquid into a small bowl. To roast pepper, set pepper directly on gas burner or place under broiler; cook and turn until skin is charred on all sides. Let cool in a closed paper bag. Use a sharp knife to remove charred skin.

SHRIMP IN COCONUT CURRY SAUCE

Easy, elegant and ever-so-exotic, this stunning dish is quick to prepare and can be served hot or warm. Unsweetened coconut milk is increasingly available in supermarkets. Select mild or hot curry powder according to your taste.

Preparation time: 15 minutes
Cooking time: 25 minutes
Yield: 8 servings

$1/4$ cup ($1/2$ stick) **unsalted butter or olive oil**

2 pounds medium shrimp, peeled, deveined

2 medium onions, chopped

4 teaspoons minced fresh ginger

2 large cloves garlic, minced

3 to 4 teaspoons curry powder to taste

2 cans (14 ounces each) unsweetened coconut milk

1 cup whipping cream or milk

$1/4$ **teaspoon salt**

$1/8$ **teaspoon cayenne**

Chopped fresh cilantro

1. Heat half of the butter in large heavy-bottomed skillet. When hot, add half of the shrimp in a single layer. Cook over medium-high heat until shrimp just turn pink and are cooked through, about 4 minutes. Remove to a bowl. Repeat with remaining butter to cook remaining shrimp. Remove shrimp to the bowl.

2. Add onions, ginger and garlic to pan. Cook and stir until softened, about 5 minutes. Stir in curry powder; cook and stir 2 minutes. Stir in coconut milk; heat to a boil while scraping up cooked bits from bottom of pan until milk is slightly reduced. Stir in cream and boil gently until reduced enough to lightly coat the back of a spoon, about 5 minutes. Add salt and cayenne. Taste and adjust seasonings.

3. Push mixture through a fine wire-mesh strainer into a bowl. Recipe can be made ahead to this point. Reheat sauce gently in a clean pan; add shrimp to reheat briefly. Spoon sauce onto individual plates. Top with shrimp. Garnish with cilantro.

STEAMED SHU MAI WITH DIPPING SAUCE

These Cantonese-style dumplings, filled with chicken and mushrooms,
are steamed rather than fried.
They make the New Year's celebration a dim sum feast.

Preparation time: 45 minutes
Cooking time: 10 minutes
Yield: About 2 dozen

STEAMED SHU MAI

4 dried shiitake or Chinese black mushrooms

3 boneless chicken breast halves, skinned, cut in 1-inch pieces

3 green onions, minced

1 small carrot, peeled, minced

2 tablespoons dry sherry

2 teaspoons each: oyster sauce, cornstarch

1$^{1}/_{2}$ teaspoons soy sauce

1 teaspoon each: Oriental sesame oil, minced fresh ginger

2 dozen won ton wrappers

1. For filling, soak mushrooms in hot water to cover until soft, about 20 minutes. Drain; discard stems. Finely chop caps. Put chicken into food processor or blender. Process with on/off turns until finely ground. Mix ground chicken, mushrooms and remaining ingredients except won ton wrappers in medium bowl.

GRAZING CELEBRATION FOR SIX

Bite-size egg rolls

Steamed shu mai

Dipping sauce

Mini ribs

East-West sesame chicken with broccoli

Steamed rice

Fortune cookies

Chinese beer and tea

2. Use a round cookie cutter to cut circles from won ton wrappers. Put about 1 heaping teaspoon of the filling onto center of each circle. Moisten edges of wrapper slightly with water. Gather up edges of circle to crimp wrapper around filling but still leaving filling showing at the top.

3. Put dumplings into a steamer basket. Set basket over wok half-filled with boiling water. Steam, covered, until filling is opaque, about 10 minutes. Serve with dipping sauce.

DIPPING SAUCE

$^{1}/_{2}$ cup soy sauce

$^{1}/_{4}$ cup: rice vinegar, dry sherry

2 teaspoons sugar

2 to 3 teaspoons chili paste with garlic or hot chili oil

Mix all ingredients in small bowl.

EAST-WEST SESAME CHICKEN WITH BROCCOLI

Several years ago, the Food Guide *asked chefs to approach the microwave oven
with an open mind and concoct some easy, clever and tasty uses for it.
John Terczak, now the owner of Tamales Restaurant in Chicago, came up
with this recipe, an explosion of flavor and color and a marvel of simplicity.*

Preparation time: 30 minutes
Microwave cooking time:
   10 to 12 minutes
Yield: 4 to 6 servings

**1 bunch green onions, chopped,
about $^3/_4$ cup**

1 cup chicken stock or broth

2 tablespoons Oriental sesame oil

**1 tablespoon each: minced garlic,
minced fresh ginger, extra-virgin
olive oil**

$^1/_2$ pound mushrooms, sliced

**2 whole chicken breasts, skinned,
boned, split, cut into bite-size
pieces**

**Salt, freshly ground black pepper
to taste**

2 cups broccoli flowerets

**$^1/_2$ red bell pepper, diced
into $^3/_4$-inch pieces, about $^1/_2$ cup**

1 box (6 ounces) frozen pea pods

2$^1/_2$ teaspoons cornstarch

2 tablespoons butter, softened

**$^1/_4$ teaspoon each: black and white
sesame seeds**

1 bunch watercress for garnish

1. Reserve about 2 tablespoons of
the green onions for garnish. Put
remaining green onions in food
processor with chicken stock,
sesame oil, garlic and ginger. Process
until almost smooth.

2. Put olive oil in skillet over high
heat; cook mushrooms until lightly
browned. Remove from heat.

3. Put chicken in 2-quart
microwave-safe casserole. Season
with salt and pepper. Add broccoli,
red pepper and pea pods. Pour in
green onion sauce. Cover with
plastic wrap vented at one corner.
Microwave on high (100 percent)
power, stirring at least twice, until
chicken is cooked and vegetables are
crisp-tender, 7 to 9 minutes. Let
stand, covered, 5 minutes.

4. Using a slotted spoon, arrange
chicken and vegetables on a serving
platter. Cover with plastic wrap to
keep warm.

5. Stir cornstarch into cooking juices
in casserole. Microwave on high,
stirring twice, until smooth and
thickened, about 3 minutes. Stir in
butter; taste and adjust seasonings
with salt and pepper. Pour sauce
over chicken mixture. Sprinkle with
sesame seeds and reserved green
onions. Garnish with watercress.

LOBSTER SALAD WITH AVOCADO MAYONNAISE

The best Valentine's celebrations are for two, making something as extravagant as lobster more affordable. Joanne McInerney-Lubeck, owner of Fresh Starts Restaurant and Catering in Flossmoor, Illinois, came up with this sumptuous, sexy salad. The mood-setting drink of choice is champagne.

Preparation time: 30 minutes
Cooking time: 6 minutes
Yield: 2 servings

LOBSTER

1 large or 2 small lobster tails

1 1/4 cups dry white wine

1/4 cup each: raspberry-flavored liqueur, water

1 leek, white part only, chopped

Juice of 1 lemon

RASPBERRY VINAIGRETTE

2/3 cup walnut oil

1/3 cup raspberry vinegar

1/4 cup raspberry puree (see note)

1 tablespoon sugar

1/4 teaspoon white pepper

SALAD

4 cups torn assorted salad greens

1 ripe avocado, peeled, sliced

1 large grapefruit, peeled, sectioned

1/4 cup shredded red cabbage

AVOCADO MAYONNAISE

1/2 ripe avocado

1/4 cup mayonnaise

Salt, pepper to taste

1. Thaw lobster tails if frozen. Put wine, liqueur, water, leek and lemon juice into medium saucepan. Heat to simmer. Add lobster tails; return to simmer. Simmer until lobster is pink

DINNER FOR TWO

Herbed brie

Lobster salad with avocado mayonnaise

Whole wheat rolls

Cappuccino chocolate heart cakes

Champagne

and meat is opaque, 4 to 6 minutes depending on size. Drain; cool lobster. Remove from shell and slice into rounds.

2. For raspberry vinaigrette, put all ingredients into jar with tight-fitting lid. Shake well.

3. For salad, arrange salad greens on serving plates. Arrange lobster slices, avocado slices and grapefruit sections over greens. Put a small pile of red cabbage in center of salad.

4. For avocado mayonnaise, mash avocado with mayonnaise in small bowl. Stir in salt and pepper.

5. Serve salad with a dollop of avocado mayonnaise in middle. Drizzle with raspberry vinaigrette. Pass remaining vinaigrette. Serve immediately.

Note: For raspberry puree, push 1/2 cup fresh or thawed frozen raspberries through a fine sieve to extract the seeds.

CAPPUCCINO CHOCOLATE HEART CAKES

*What possibly could be sweeter than small coffee-flavored chocolate hearts?
They're easily made and the only special equipment called for is a heart-shaped
cookie cutter. Extra hearts can be frozen for later indulgence.*

Preparation time: 1 hour
Cooking time: 40 minutes
Yield: 9 hearts

CAKE

1$^1/_4$ cups cake flour

$^1/_2$ cup unsweetened Dutch process cocoa

1 teaspoon each: baking soda, ground cinnamon

$^1/_2$ teaspoon salt

$^1/_4$ teaspoon baking powder

$^1/_2$ cup (1 stick) plus 2 tablespoons unsalted butter, softened

1$^1/_2$ cups granulated sugar

3 large eggs

$^1/_2$ cup buttermilk

$^1/_2$ cup very strong coffee or espresso

2 teaspoons pure vanilla extract

FOR GARNISH

$^1/_2$ teaspoon instant espresso powder

1 tablespoon confectioners' sugar

2 ounces each: semisweet chocolate, white chocolate

Fresh raspberries

1. Heat oven to 375 degrees. Butter a 9-inch-square cake pan. Line the bottom with parchment paper and butter the paper.

2. For cake, sift flour, cocoa, baking soda, cinnamon, salt and baking powder together 3 times. Beat butter and sugar in large bowl of electric mixer until light and fluffy. Beat in eggs, one at a time, beating well after each addition. Mix buttermilk, coffee and vanilla in glass measure. Alternately fold dry mixture and buttermilk mixture into egg mixture.

3. Transfer batter to prepared pan. Smooth top. Bake until top springs back when touched lightly, 35 to 40 minutes. Cool on wire rack for 10 minutes. Turn out of pan and cool completely on wire rack. Remove paper.

4. Use a heart-shaped cookie cutter, about 2$^1/_2$ inches at its widest point, to cut out heart shapes. To garnish, mix espresso powder and confectioners' sugar in small bowl. Using a fine wire-mesh strainer, sprinkle sugar mixture generously over top of hearts. Place hearts on individual serving plates.

5. Melt semisweet and white chocolate separately in small glass microwave-safe bowls in microwave oven on low (30 percent) power, stirring frequently, 1 to 2 minutes. Use the tines of a fork to drizzle melted semisweet chocolate and then white chocolate over the hearts and their plates. Garnish with raspberries.

GINGER-MUSTARD SALMON WITH LEMON SAUCE

Waters around the Emerald Isle teem with salmon, ensuring that Irish cooks find many uses for the mild, pink-fleshed fish. Here, a tart lemony sauce is a fine foil for the fish's rich taste. Searing the fish in a hot skillet and finishing it in the oven is especially easy and foolproof, but in warmer weather, the lure of the grill can be succumbed to as well.

Preparation time: 20 minutes
Marinating time: 30 minutes or more
Cooking time: 12 minutes
Yield: 4 servings

MARINADE

1 piece fresh ginger, about 1-inch cube, peeled

1 teaspoon grated lemon rind

3 tablespoons each: fresh lemon juice, vegetable oil

2 tablespoons honey

2 teaspoons each: grainy mustard, soy sauce

$1/2$ teaspoon salt

4 salmon fillets, 6 to 7 ounces each

SAUCE

$1/2$ cup dry white wine

1 tablespoon seasoned or plain rice vinegar

1 large shallot, minced

1 teaspoon dried rosemary

3 tablespoons whipping cream

2 tablespoons cold unsalted butter

Salt, freshly ground white pepper to taste

Fresh chives, optional

1. For the marinade, mince ginger with lemon rind in a food processor or blender. Add lemon juice, 2 tablespoons of the oil, honey, mustard, soy sauce and salt; mix well. Reserve half of the marinade to use for the sauce.

PARTY FOR FOUR

Watercress salad

Ginger-mustard salmon with lemon sauce

Fried potatoes and cabbage

Soda bread

Irish whiskey oat cake

Irish beer

Transfer the rest to a large plastic food bag and add salmon. Refrigerate at least 30 minutes or as long as 8 hours.

2. Heat oven to 450 degrees. Heat remaining 1 tablespoon oil in a heavy, ovenproof skillet, preferably cast-iron, over high heat. Add salmon, skin side down, and cook 3 minutes. Transfer to the oven; cook just until cooked through, 5 to 6 minutes.

3. Begin the sauce while the salmon is cooking. Combine wine, vinegar, the shallot and rosemary in a small non-aluminum pan. Boil over high heat until it is reduced to 3 tablespoons, 6 to 8 minutes. Add reserved marinade and cream. Reduce to 6 tablespoons. Turn heat to low. Cut the butter into 2 pieces. Whisk them in, one at a time, waiting until the first piece is incorporated before adding the other. Add salt and pepper to taste. Sauce can be made a day ahead and gently reheated on the stovetop or using medium (50 percent) power in a microwave oven.

4. Strain sauce over fish. Garnish with chives, if desired.

IRISH WHISKEY OAT CAKE

The simple becomes sublime when oats are soaked in a lavish amount of Irish whiskey before using them in this currant-studded cake. Water can be used in place of the whiskey although both the texture and taste will be different.

Preparation time: 30 minutes
Standing time: 20 minutes
Cooking time: 45 minutes
Yield: One 9-inch cake

CAKE

$^1/_2$ cup Irish whiskey

1 cup old-fashioned rolled oats

$^1/_2$ cup dried currants or raisins

1$^1/_3$ cups all-purpose flour

1 teaspoon baking soda

$^1/_2$ teaspoon each: salt, nutmeg, allspice

1$^1/_4$ cups granulated sugar

$^1/_2$ cup packed light brown sugar

$^2/_3$ cup solid vegetable shortening

2 large eggs

1 tablespoon molasses

2 teaspoons pure vanilla extract

TOPPING

1 cup whipping cream

2 tablespoons confectioners' sugar

2 teaspoons Irish whiskey

1 teaspoon pure vanilla extract

1. For cake, put whiskey, oats and currants in a bowl; let stand 20 minutes. Mix flour, baking soda, salt, nutmeg and allspice; set aside. Heat oven to 350 degrees. Grease a 9-inch springform pan.

2. Beat granulated sugar, brown sugar and shortening in large bowl of an electric mixer on high speed until light, about 2 minutes. Beat in eggs, one at a time, mixing well after each addition. Mix in oat mixture, molasses and vanilla. Fold in dry ingredients.

3. Transfer batter to prepared pan. Bake until a toothpick inserted in center comes out clean, about 45 minutes. Cool on a wire rack. Loosen cake from sides of pan; remove sides.

4. For topping, whip cream in small bowl of electric mixer until it holds soft peaks. Add confectioners' sugar, whiskey and vanilla and mix to combine. Serve cake warm or at room temperature, sprinkled with confectioners' sugar and topped with whipped cream.

FETTUCCINE ALLA PRIMAVERA

Spring is the inspiration for this lovely pairing of tender young vegetables with a tangle of pasta. Michael Monteleone, a Chicago produce distributor, shared this version of a classic dish. Not too surprisingly, he puts extra emphasis on the vegetables and suggests improvising with what's seasonal and best in the market.

Preparation time: 45 minutes
Cooking time: 15 minutes
Yield: 12 first-course servings

---

1 bunch thin asparagus, ends trimmed

1¹/₂ cups fresh fiddlehead ferns, rinsed, optional

1¹/₂ cups peeled baby carrots, julienned

1¹/₂ cups French or small green beans, ends trimmed

1¹/₂ cups small fresh sugar snap or snow pea pods, strings removed

3 tablespoons extra-virgin olive oil

SAUCE

1¹/₂ tablespoons each: butter, flour

1¹/₂ cups whipping cream or milk, heated

2 cloves garlic, pressed

¹/₄ teaspoon freshly ground nutmeg

Salt, freshly ground pepper to taste

1¹/₂ pounds fettuccine noodles

8-10 fresh basil leaves, sliced into thin ribbons

Freshly grated imported Romano cheese

Fresh basil sprigs for garnish

CELEBRATION FOR TWELVE

Fettuccine alla primavera

Jalapeno-crusted ham with caramelized onions

Steamed artichoke halves

Whipped sweet potatoes

Hot cross buns

Strawberry shortcake

Sauvignon blanc

1. Cut asparagus into 1-inch pieces. Reserve the tips. Drop stalks into boiling water; cook 1 minute. Add the asparagus tips and the fiddlehead ferns if using; cook 1 more minute. Drain; rinse under cold water. Cook carrots, beans and peas in boiling water until crisp-tender, 1 to 3 minutes. Drain; rinse under cold water. Toss vegetables together with olive oil.

2. For sauce, melt butter in small, heavy saucepan. Stir in flour; cook and stir 1 minute. Gradually whisk in hot cream. Cook, stirring constantly, until smooth and thick. Stir in garlic, nutmeg, salt and pepper. Taste and adjust seasonings. Cover and keep warm.

3. Cook fettuccine in boiling water according to package directions until al dente. Drain; put into large bowl. Add sauce and vegetables; toss to coat all with sauce. Transfer to serving platter. Sprinkle with ribbons of basil and grated cheese. Garnish with basil sprigs.

JALAPENO-CRUSTED HAM WITH CARAMELIZED ONIONS

Ham continues its long-running reign as king of the Easter table and leaner varieties ensure that this will continue. Here, the crisscross pattern of cloves is dealt aside in favor of a sassy sweet-hot topping of breadcrumbs and jalapeno jelly. Bronzed caramelized onions are served alongside.

Preparation time: 30 minutes
Cooking time: 3½ hours
Yield: 12 to 16 servings

---

1 fully-cooked smoked ham, about 12 pounds

2 pints each: white pearl onions, red pearl onions

3 tablespoons each: unsalted butter, vegetable oil

¼ teaspoon sugar

1 jalapeno chili pepper, seeded or minced, or ½ teaspoon crushed red pepper flakes

Salt to taste

½ cup (1 stick) unsalted butter

4 cups fresh homemade coarse bread crumbs, from bread such as egg twist

¼ cup chopped fresh cilantro or parsley

½ cup hot pepper jelly, about

1. Heat oven to 325 degrees. Put ham into a large, shallow roasting pan. Bake ham until meat thermometer inserted in thickest part away from bone registers 140 degrees, 15 to 18 minutes per pound, about 3 to 3½ hours.

2. Meanwhile, for caramelized onions, add pearl onions to large pot of boiling water. Cook just until skins loosen and onions are slightly softened, 3 to 5 minutes. Drain; slip off skins.

3. Heat 3 tablespoons butter and oil in large heavy skillet. Add onions; cook, shaking pan frequently, until onions are golden on all sides, about 8 minutes. Add sugar; stir to mix; continue to cook until onions are nicely browned, about 4 minutes. Sprinkle with minced jalapeno and salt. Remove from heat.

4. Remove the ham to a cutting board. While still warm, trim off all the brown rind and most of the fat, leaving a thin ⅛-inch layer all around. Put ham back into clean roasting pan.

5. Heat oven to 500 degrees. Melt ½ cup butter in large nonstick skillet. Add bread crumbs; cook and stir over medium-low heat until butter is absorbed and crumbs are slightly crisped, about 3 minutes. Remove from heat; stir in cilantro.

6. Coat ham liberally with jelly. Using your hands, press crumbs into jelly to completely cover ham. Bake at 500 degrees just until crumbs are crisp, about 15 minutes. Serve the ham thinly sliced accompanied by the onions. The ham will stay warm, loosely covered, for about 1 hour. It also can be served cold.

HOT CROSS BUNS

Steeped in the lore of Easter, these sweet, spiced, fruit-studded buns often come to the Lenten table at breakfast time. They make a fine addition to the dinner meal, though, especially good with the pepper-glazed ham. Their tradition suggests shaping the dough into rolls and slashing a cross into each one. A timewise alternative is to make a single loaf.

Preparation time: 45 minutes
Rising time: About 3 hours
Cooking time: 15 to 20 minutes
Yield: About 2 dozen

---

1 package active dry yeast

$1/4$ cup very warm water (105 to 115 degrees)

Pinch sugar

$3/4$ cup plain yogurt, at room temperature

$1/3$ cup granulated sugar

1 teaspoon salt

$1/4$ cup ($1/2$ stick) unsalted butter, softened

2 large eggs

1 teaspoon ground cinnamon

$1/2$ teaspoon freshly ground nutmeg

$3^1/2$ cups all-purpose flour, about

1 cup currants

1 egg yolk

2 tablespoons whipping cream or milk

GLAZE

$1^1/2$ cups confectioners' sugar

2 to 3 tablespoons fresh orange juice

1. Mix yeast, water and a pinch of sugar in large bowl of electric mixer fitted with a dough hook. Let stand until bubbly, about 5 minutes. Mix yogurt, $1/3$ cup sugar, salt, butter, eggs, cinnamon and nutmeg in small bowl. Add to yeast mixture; mix well.

2. Mix in enough of flour to form a soft, slightly sticky dough. Knead on low speed until smooth and elastic, about 10 minutes.

3. Put dough into a buttered bowl. Turn to butter the other side. Let rise, covered with a clean towel, in a warm place until doubled, about $1^1/2$ hours.

4. Punch down dough. Knead in currants until they are evenly dispersed throughout the dough.

Return to the buttered bowl. Let rise, covered, a second time until doubled, about 1 hour.

5. Punch down dough and turn out onto floured surface. Pat dough to $1/2$-inch thickness. Cut dough with a lightly floured round cutter, about 2 inches in diameter. Put onto greased baking sheets about 1 inch apart. Reroll scraps and cut to use up all the dough.

6. Let rise, covered, until almost doubled, about 30 minutes.

7. Heat oven to 375 degrees. Just before baking, use floured scissors to snip a cross on top of each bun. Beat egg yolk and cream and brush lightly over tops of buns. Bake until golden, about 15 to 20 minutes. Cool on wire rack until warm.

8. When cooled, mix confectioners' sugar and orange juice to a thick drizzling consistency. Using a spoon, drizzle a cross over each bun. Serve warm.

STRAWBERRY SHORTCAKE

Strawberry shortcake is the dessert of desserts, a feast for the eyes as well as the taste buds, especially when fresh, locally grown berries at the height of the season are used. The recipe can be halved.

Preparation time: 1 hour
Cooking time: 25 minutes
Yield: 12 servings

SHORTCAKE

4 cups all-purpose flour

6 tablespoons sugar

4 teaspoons baking powder

$^1/_2$ teaspoon salt

$1^1/_4$ cups ($2^1/_2$ sticks) cold unsalted butter, cut into pieces

$1^1/_3$ cups milk

STRAWBERRY MIXTURE

8 cups small strawberries, rinsed, hulled

$^3/_4$ cup sugar

2 tablespoons orange-flavored liqueur

WHIPPED CREAM

3 cups cold whipping cream

6 tablespoons granulated sugar

Confectioners' sugar

Fresh mint leaves for garnish

1. Heat oven to 400 degrees. Have ungreased baking sheets ready.

2. For shortcake biscuits, put flour, sugar, baking powder and salt into food processor. Process to mix. Add butter; process until mixture resembles coarse crumbs. Add milk; process just until dough gathers. Do not overmix. (To make by hand, mix dry ingredients in large bowl; cut in butter with pastry blender or two knives until coarse crumbs form; add milk; toss with fork until dough gathers.)

3. Transfer dough to a well-floured work surface. Roll lightly to about 1-inch thickness. Cut with floured 3-inch biscuit cutter into 12 biscuits. (When rerolling scraps, work dough as little as possible.) Put onto baking sheets. Bake until tops are golden, 20 to 25 minutes. Cool on wire rack.

4. While biscuits bake, prepare strawberries. Puree $^1/_2$ cup of the strawberries in food processor or blender. Cut remaining strawberries in half if large. Put into large bowl; add strawberry puree, sugar and liqueur. Mix well. Let marinate at least 30 minutes or up to several hours in the refrigerator.

5. Using chilled beaters, whip cream in a large chilled bowl until soft peaks form. Beat in granulated sugar.

6. To assemble, split warm biscuits in half. Sprinkle tops of biscuits with confectioners' sugar. Put bottoms onto serving plates. Top with a generous amount of the strawberries and then some of the whipped cream. Put top of biscuits over whipped cream and spoon a little more cream on top. Garnish with mint leaves and serve immediately.

CHICKEN MARBELLA

This was the first main-course dish to be offered at the Silver Palate, the famous takeout food shop in New York. Its distinctive colors and bold mix of flavors made it a favorite there for years. After it appeared in the Food Guide, *many readers adopted it as an instant family classic. The cooked chicken keeps and even improves after a day of refrigeration. The recipe is adapted from* The Silver Palate Cookbook.

Preparation time: 30 minutes
Marinating time: Overnight
Cooking time: 50 to 60 minutes
Yield: 10 servings

---

4 chickens, 2^1/2 pounds each, quartered

1 cup pitted prunes

^{1}/2 cup each: pitted Spanish green olives, capers with a bit of juice

^{1}/2 cup each: red wine vinegar, olive oil

1 head of garlic, peeled, pureed

^{1}/4 cup dried oregano

6 bay leaves

Coarse (kosher) salt, freshly ground black pepper to taste

1 cup each: packed brown sugar, white wine

^{1}/4 cup fresh Italian parsley or cilantro, finely chopped

1. Combine chicken quarters, prunes, olives, capers with juice, vinegar, olive oil, garlic puree, oregano, bay leaves, and salt and pepper to taste in a large bowl. Cover and refrigerate overnight, turning chicken occasionally.

2. Heat oven to 350 degrees. Arrange chicken in a single layer in one or two large, shallow baking pans and spoon marinade over it evenly. Sprinkle chicken pieces with brown sugar and pour white wine around them.

SEDER FOR TEN

Chicken Marbella

Sesame asparagus with diced peppers and fennel

Spinach salad with red onions

Matzoh

Almond-raisin matzoh kugel

Sponge cake with sliced strawberries

Kosher wine

3. Bake, basting frequently with pan juices, until thigh pieces, when pierced with a fork at their thickest point, yield clear yellow (rather than pink) juices, 50 to 60 minutes.

4. Transfer chicken, prunes, olives and capers to a serving platter with a slotted spoon. Moisten with a few spoonfuls of pan juices and sprinkle generously with parsley or cilantro. Pass remaining pan juices in a sauceboat.

Note: To make ahead and serve at room temperature, refrigerate chicken in cooking juices. Allow it to return to room temperature before arranging on serving platter. Spoon some of the reserved juice over chicken; sprinkle with parsley.

SESAME ASPARAGUS WITH DICED PEPPERS AND FENNEL

A lighter, easier approach is redefining the Passover meal in many families. This colorful and vibrant-flavored asparagus preparation from Abby Mandel answers the call in grand style. It can be served as a first course or as a vegetable side dish. Bulb fennel, hard to find in some areas, can be replaced with celery.

Preparation time: 20 minutes
Cooking time: 10 minutes
Yield: 8 to 10 servings

---

3 pounds medium asparagus, about 36 spears, trimmed

5 tablespoons sesame oil

1 tablespoon vegetable oil

1 medium bulb fennel, trimmed, diced into $1/4$-inch pieces

1 each, diced into $1/4$-inch pieces: red bell pepper, yellow bell pepper

5 tablespoons vinegar

$1/2$ teaspoon sugar

2 large green onions, thinly sliced

Salt, crushed red pepper flakes to taste

$1/4$ cup minced fresh cilantro

1. Cook asparagus in large kettle of boiling salted water until tender but not soft, about 6 minutes. Drain in colander; rinse under cold water to keep green color.

2. Heat oils in large skillet over medium-high heat. When very hot, add fennel and peppers. Cook until heated through, about 2 minutes. Add vinegar and sugar. Heat through, about 2 more minutes, tossing ingredients in pan. Remove from heat. Add green onions, salt and red pepper flakes. Pour over asparagus on serving platter. Garnish with cilantro.

CHICKEN ALMOND SALAD WITH TARRAGON DRESSING

For all its simplicity, chicken salad is a classic that is equally at home in a corner diner, a chic restaurant or a lunchtime meal honoring Mother's Day. A helpful strategy that many cooks rely on is to cook an extra chicken and count on the leftovers for a salad the next day.

Preparation time: 30 minutes
Cooking time: 1 hour
Chilling time: Several hours
   or overnight
Yield: 4 to 6 servings

---

1 broiler/fryer chicken, 3 to 3^1/$_2$ pounds

^{2}/$_3$ cup homemade or good-quality mayonnaise

2 tablespoons sour cream or plain yogurt

1 tablespoon each: grainy Dijon mustard, lime juice

2 tablespoons minced fresh tarragon or 1^1/$_2$ teaspoons dried

^{1}/$_8$ teaspoon cayenne pepper

Salt, freshly ground white pepper to taste

3 to 4 ounces blanched, sliced almonds

1^1/$_2$ cups diced celery

2 tablespoons finely chopped parsley

Green and red leaf lettuce, for serving

Fresh tarragon sprigs, cherry tomatoes for garnish

1. Heat oven to 350 degrees. Wash chicken, removing giblets and neck for other use. Pat dry and place in roasting pan, breast-side down. Cook 30 minutes, turn chicken and continue roasting another 30 minutes, or until juices run clear when thickest part of drumstick is pierced with fork. Remove from oven; let stand until cool enough to handle.

LUNCHEON FOR FOUR

Chicken almond salad with tarragon dressing

Sugar snap peas

Cheese muffins or croissants

Anise and orange poached pears

Iced tea with lemon

2. Mix mayonnaise, sour cream, mustard, lime juice, tarragon, cayenne, salt and pepper in small bowl. Whisk together until smooth.

3. To toast almonds, put almonds into small nonstick or well-seasoned skillet. Cook, shaking pan constantly over medium heat, until almonds are lightly toasted. Immediately remove from pan to a plate to cool.

4. Pull chicken off bones, discarding bones and skin. Cut chicken into chunks. Mix chicken, celery, parsley and the dressing, tossing to blend. Sprinkle almonds over salad and chill, covered, for several hours or overnight to blend flavors. Serve salad on a bed of green and red lettuce leaves. Garnish with fresh tarragon and tomatoes.

ANISE AND ORANGE POACHED PEARS

Poached pears often are overlooked as a dessert option. But they are extremely easy and foolproof to prepare, light, low in fat and calories and can be made ahead of time, all good reasons to consider them. Most importantly, they make a stunning presentation and taste sensational. This version is from free-lance writer Andrew Schloss.

Preparation time: 30 minutes
Cooking time: 35 to 45 minutes
Yield: 4 servings

---

1 cup each: fresh orange juice, white wine

$1/2$ cup each: water, sugar

$1/3$ cup anise-flavored liqueur such as Pernod or Sambuca

1 tablespoon fruit vinegar such as raspberry

1 vanilla bean

4 slightly underripe Anjou or Bartlett pears, peeled, cored

Julienned rind of 1 orange

$1/8$ teaspoon pure anise extract, optional

1. Combine the orange juice, wine, water, sugar, liqueur, vinegar and vanilla bean in a high-sided non-aluminum saucepan just large enough to hold the pears upright. Heat to a boil.

2. Add the pears and reduce heat to a simmer. Cover; cook until pears are tender enough to pierce easily with the tip of a sharp knife, 15 to 25 minutes. Cooking time varies depending on how ripe the pears are. If the pears are not completely submerged in the poaching liquid, turn them every few minutes so they cook evenly. When the pears are uniformly tender, remove from heat and cool in the liquid.

3. Before serving, remove the pears from the liquid and stand upright on individual plates. Remove the vanilla bean; add orange rind to the liquid. Cook over medium heat until liquid reduces to $1/2$ to $3/4$ cup, about 20 minutes. Add the anise extract; pour liquid over the pears.

TORTILLA SOUP WITH AVOCADO

Cinco de Mayo officially commemorates a Mexican victory in battle and unofficially gives cause for a festive celebration that is dearly loved by Mexicans. An offbeat soup-and-sandwich menu, partnered with cold beer or margaritas, is a grand way to celebrate. The soup, made from a deceptively simple collection of ingredients—including stale tortillas—is transformed into a marvelously complex soup that bursts with character.

Preparation time: 20 minutes
Cooking time: 30 minutes
Yield: 6 servings

---

8 stale corn tortillas

Vegetable oil

2 large dried pasilla chilies

1 large ripe tomato

1 clove garlic

¹/₂ small white onion

6 cups chicken stock or broth

2 tablespoons minced fresh cilantro

Salt, freshly ground pepper to taste

1 avocado, peeled, sliced

Grated anejo or Parmesan cheese

Fresh lime wedges

1. Cut tortillas into thin strips. Heat ¹/₄-inch oil in large skillet until hot. Fry tortilla strips, a few at a time, until crisp and golden. Remove with slotted spoon. Drain on paper towels. Add dried chilies to same oil. Fry until puffed and crisp, about 30 seconds. Drain on paper towels; remove stems and seeds; crumble chilies.

2. Drain all oil from pan but do not wipe pan clean. Add tomato, garlic and onion to pan. Cook over medium-high heat, turning, to lightly char exterior of tomato, garlic and onion. Remove core from tomato. Put vegetables into blender container. Blend, adding some of the chicken stock as needed, until smooth.

3. Put tomato mixture and remaining chicken stock into large saucepan. Simmer, stirring often, for 20 minutes. Stir in cilantro. Taste and add salt and pepper as needed.

4. To serve, ladle broth mixture into hot serving bowls. Drop tortilla pieces, crumbled chilies, sliced avocado and grated cheese into soup. Squeeze a bit of lime juice over, stir once and serve immediately.

SUPPER FOR SIX

Tortilla soup with avocado

Roast pork sandwiches on bolillos

Sliced tomatoes

Mangoes with lime juice

Assorted beers or margaritas

ROAST PORK SANDWICHES ON BOLILLOS

While tacos may be the most familiar form of Mexican "sandwiches," tortas are very popular throughout Mexico and in Hispanic communities in the States. Made with bolillos, torpedo-shaped hard rolls, they are filled with endless permutations of meat, cheese, refried beans and salsa. Here, savory roast pork is featured.

Preparation time: 25 minutes
Cooking time: 35 minutes
Yield: 6 servings

---

1 large clove garlic, cut into slivers

1 pork tenderloin, about ³/₄ pound

Vegetable oil

Coarsely ground black pepper

**6 large or 12 small bolillos
or hard rolls**

1 cup refried beans

Leaf lettuce

Thinly sliced red onion

Sliced tomatoes

**Shredded Monterey jack
or brick cheese**

Sprigs fresh cilantro

Salsa

1. Heat oven to 375 degrees. Using a small paring knife, insert slivers of garlic into tenderloin at even intervals. Rub tenderloin with oil then coat liberally with black pepper. Put into small roasting pan. Roast until meat thermometer inserted in thickest portion registers 150 degrees, 25 to 35 minutes. Cool 10 minutes before carving into very thin slices.

2. To assemble sandwiches, cut rolls in half. Spread a thin layer of beans on each half. Layer lettuce, onion, sliced pork, tomatoes, cheese and cilantro on bottom halves. Top with a dollop of salsa. Sandwich with top halves of rolls.

BISTRO STEAK WITH HERBED BUTTER

A grilled steak is as all-American as it gets. But add a dab of flavored butter and a side of pommes frites — French fries — and it becomes a French bistro classic. The grill is Dad's domain, so likely he'll do the honors. Other preparations can be part of a group effort, with everyone lending a hand to make Dad's day special.

Preparation time: 15 minutes
Cooking time: 10 minutes
Yield: 4 servings

---

4 oil-cured green olives, pitted

2 sprigs parsley

1 shallot

1 small clove garlic

¹/₄ cup (¹/₂ stick) unsalted butter, softened

1¹/₂ teaspoons Dijon mustard

¹/₄ teaspoon freshly ground black pepper

Salt to taste

4 boneless beef top loin steaks (strip steaks), about 6 ounces each, trimmed

1. Finely chop olives, parsley, shallot and garlic in food processor or blender. Add butter, mustard, pepper and salt; process until well mixed. Scrape mixture out onto a sheet of waxed paper. Using the paper, shape the butter mixture into a log and refrigerate it until firm or up to several days.

2. Prepare a charcoal grill or heat broiler. Grill or broil steaks, 6 inches from heat source, turning once, until medium-rare, 8 to 10 minutes.

3. Put steaks onto serving plates. Top each with a thin slice or two of the herbed butter. The heat of the steak will melt the butter. Serve immediately.

BISTRO DINNER FOR FOUR

Assorted pâtés

Bistro steak with herbed butter

French fries

Stuffed tomato

Watercress salad

French bread

Apple charlotte with Calvados

Cabernet Sauvignon or beer

APPLE CHARLOTTE WITH CALVADOS

Many a father names apple pie as his favorite dessert. Here, some of the same basic ingredients are put together in an entirely different manner. Although the charlotte looks complicated, it is quite easy to make and doesn't require the meticulous skills of a pastry chef. If you don't have a charlotte mold, a deep, straight-sided oven-proof bowl will do just fine.

Preparation time: 45 minutes
Cooking time: 40 minutes
Yield: 4 servings

---

3 tablespoons dark raisins

2 tablespoons Calvados (apple brandy) or Applejack

8 tablespoons (1 stick) unsalted butter

8 slices day-old high-quality white bread

4 or 5 tart apples, such as Granny Smith, peeled, cored, cut into $1/2$-inch slices

3 tablespoons granulated sugar

1 teaspoon vanilla extract

$1/2$ cup whipping cream

1 tablespoon confectioners' sugar

1. Heat oven to 375 degrees. Spoon the raisins into a small bowl. Add the Calvados, stir and set aside.

2. Heat 3 tablespoons of the butter in a large skillet. Add the bread slices in a single layer. Cook, turning once, until light gold on both sides. Add more butter to pan if needed.

3. Heat 2 more tablespoons of butter in the skillet. Add half the apple slices, cover and cook until apples are tender but not mushy, about 5 minutes. Transfer apples and pan juices to a mixing bowl; sprinkle with granulated sugar and $1/2$ teaspoon of the vanilla. Add 2 more tablespoons of butter to the pan and cook the remaining apples. Add to the bowl.

4. Rub the sides and bottom of a 1-quart charlotte mold with the remaining 1 tablespoon of butter. Cut enough toasted bread into triangles and small filler pieces to line the bottom of the mold. Cut the remaining bread slices in half, and line the sides of the mold. Trim the bread as necessary so the vertical pieces are flush with the top of the mold. Reserve the bread trimmings.

5. Put bread trimmings and any remaining bread (at least a half slice) in a food processor; process to make crumbs. Strain Calvados from the raisin bowl into the apple slices, then toss the raisins with the bread crumbs. Fill the mold with apples, then sprinkle crumb-raisin mixture over the top.

6. Place the mold on a baking sheet. Bake in center of oven for 20 minutes. Cover tightly with aluminum foil; bake 10 more minutes. Cool on a wire rack until warm.

7. Beat the cream until foamy. Beat in remaining $1/2$ teaspoon vanilla and confectioners' sugar; beat just until soft peaks form. Invert charlotte onto a serving plate; cut it into 4 wedges. Top with a dollop of cream.

GRILLED LAMBURGERS WITH RED ONIONS

Just about every survey confirms that burgers are the most popular food for grilling. This recipe acknowledges that summertime truth but expands the category a bit by using lamb in place of beef. Following the theme through, serve the burgers in pita pockets with yogurt sauce or jalapeno jelly as a relish.

Preparation time: 15 minutes
Cooking time: 8 to 10 minutes
Yield: 8 burgers

---

2 pounds lean ground lamb

2 small sweet onions, coarsely minced

2/3 cup loosely packed fresh mint leaves, minced

Generous 1/2 teaspoon salt

Freshly ground pepper to taste

2 medium red onions, thickly sliced

1. Mix lamb, minced onions, mint, salt and pepper with a fork in mixing bowl. Keep mixture light. Gently shape mixture into 8 equal burgers. Can be made several hours ahead and refrigerated, covered with plastic wrap.

2. Prepare a charcoal grill or preheat broiler. Grill or broil lamburgers and red onion slices, 6 inches from heat source, turning once, until burgers are medium-rare and onions are crisp-tender, 8 to 10 minutes. Serve immediately.

GRILL-OUT FOR EIGHT

Grilled lamburgers with red onions

Whole wheat buns or pita bread

Blue cheese macaroni salad with grapes

Grilled vegetables with tangy mustard sauce

Potato salad with sausage

Carrot sticks, sliced tomatoes

Banana splits

Lemonade

BLUE CHEESE MACARONI SALAD WITH GRAPES

Traditions are great to have but every now and then, it's fun to tamper with them and see what happens. The Food Guide *did just that when we asked Bob Burcenski, owner of Tallgrass and Public Landing in Lockport, Illinois, to noodle around with the classic summer macaroni salad. He added a few unexpected ingredients and won rave reviews for this updated version.*

Preparation time: 20 minutes
Cooking time: 15 minutes
Yield: 6 to 8 servings

---

1 package (7 ounces) elbow macaroni

1 tablespoon unsalted butter

1 cup each: coarsely chopped walnuts, mayonnaise

2 teaspoons Dijon mustard

1/2 cup each, halved: seedless red and green grapes

3 ounces blue cheese

Pepper to taste

1. Cook macaroni according to package; drain well and set aside to cool slightly in a large bowl.

2. Melt butter over medium heat in a small skillet. Add walnuts and cook, stirring often, until they are well toasted, 4 to 5 minutes. Add to macaroni.

3. Add mayonnaise, mustard and grapes and mix gently. Crumble cheese and fold in; add pepper to taste. Chill well before serving.

GRILLED VEGETABLES WITH TANGY MUSTARD SAUCE

Vegetables can cook next to the burgers on the grill and gather a wonderful charred flavor. They team well with a mustard sauce that can be made ahead. Summer squash, fennel and eggplant are good choices.

Preparation time: 25 minutes
Cooking time: 10 to 15 minutes
Yield: 8 servings

1/4 **cup Dijon mustard**

1/2 **teaspoon dry mustard**

1 **tablespoon sugar**

3/4 **cup vegetable oil**

1 1/2 **tablespoons white-wine vinegar or lemon juice**

3 **tablespoons chopped mixed fresh herbs, such as dill, tarragon or mint**

Salt, freshly ground pepper to taste

8 **small vegetables, such as eggplant, yellow squash and fresh fennel, halved**

1. For the sauce, whisk Dijon and dry mustard together in small bowl. Beat in the sugar; slowly add 1/2 cup of the vegetable oil, stirring continuously. Stir in the vinegar to taste, 1/2 tablespoon at a time. Add herbs, salt and pepper to taste. If you like, refrigerate several hours or overnight.

2. Prepare grill or preheat broiler. Brush surfaces of vegetables with remaining 1/4 cup oil; season with salt and pepper to taste. Grill vegetables 6 inches from heat source, turning, until tender, 10 to 15 minutes. Serve with mustard sauce on the side.

POTATO SALAD WITH SAUSAGE

As good as old-fashioned potato salad is, it easily can be dressed up with gourmet touches. This recipe, adapted from one served at The 95th restaurant in Chicago, adds sliced smoked sausage to a vinaigrette-dressed salad. Almost any fully-cooked sausage works, but try seeking out a lamb-and-herb sausage if serving this salad with the grilled lamburgers.

Preparation time: 30 minutes
Cooking time: 20 minutes
Yield: 8 to 10 servings

---

3 pounds medium-size red potatoes

$1/2$ pound fully-cooked smoked sausage, cut into $1/8$ -inch-thick slices

4 ribs celery, diced

$1/2$ cup sliced green onions

2 tablespoons minced Italian parsley or cilantro

DRESSING

6 tablespoons white wine tarragon vinegar

$1/2$ teaspoon each: Dijon mustard, salt, freshly ground pepper

$3/4$ cup olive oil

Lettuce leaves for serving

1. Cook potatoes in boiling water in large saucepan until just tender, 15 to 20 minutes. Drain. Cool slightly. Cut into $1/4$ -inch-thick slices.

2. Put potatoes into large bowl. Add sausage, celery, green onions and parsley. Toss gently to mix.

3. For dressing, put vinegar, mustard, salt and pepper in small bowl. Whisk to blend. Gradually whisk in oil. Pour dressing over potato mixture; toss gently to mix. Serve while still warm on a bed of lettuce leaves.

BANANA SPLITS

While Americans did not invent ice cream, we did invent the ice-cream cone, chocolate-covered ice cream on a stick, the ice-cream sundae, the ice-cream soda and the glorious banana split. These classic-style splits can be assembled ahead of time in the kitchen or at the table by the guests.

Preparation time: 25 minutes
Yield: 8 servings

---

8 small bananas, peeled

1 quart each: chocolate ice cream, vanilla ice cream, strawberry ice cream

$^1/_2$ cup each: chocolate syrup, marshmallow creme, strawberry topping

4 tablespoons drained crushed pineapple

Whipped cream, chopped nuts

8 maraschino cherries

For each split, cut 1 banana lengthwise and then crosswise in half. Arrange banana pieces in serving dish. Top with a scoop of each type of ice cream. Then top the ice cream with 1 tablespoon each of chocolate syrup, marshmallow creme and strawberry topping. Sprinkle a half tablespoon of the pineapple over all. Garnish with whipped cream, nuts and a cherry.

SPICY BEEF WITH NOODLES

Karen Levin, a Chicago-area cookbook author and food consultant, is an avid fan of Ravinia Music Festival. Good thing, too, since her back yard brushes up against the Ravinia park, where she and her family often picnic on dishes like the following Chinese-inspired entree.

Preparation time: 25 minutes
Marinating time: 15 minutes
  or overnight
Cooking time: 15 minutes
Yield: 8 servings

---

2 ounces dried Chinese mushrooms

3/4 cup peanut oil

4 teaspoons minced fresh ginger

4 large cloves garlic, minced

1 teaspoon crushed red pepper flakes

2 pounds boneless top beef sirloin, about 1 inch thick

1/4 cup each: soy sauce, rice vinegar

2 teaspoons Oriental sesame oil

2 red bell peppers, cored, cut in strips

3 cups snow peas, cut in strips

1 pound vermicelli noodles, broken in half, or somen noodles, cooked according to package directions

Chopped cashews for garnish

1. Put mushrooms in a small dish and cover with hot water; soak 20 minutes. Drain and squeeze out excess water. Cut off and discard stems; slice caps.

2. Mix 1/4 cup of the peanut oil, ginger, garlic and red pepper flakes in a small bowl. Spread 2 tablespoons of mixture evenly over both sides of meat. Marinate at room temperature for 15 minutes or refrigerate up to 24 hours. Stir 6 tablespoons of the peanut oil, soy sauce, vinegar and sesame oil into remaining oil-ginger mixture; set aside.

3. Heat a large non-stick skillet over high heat. When hot, add steak. Cook, turning once, until medium-rare, 8 to 10 minutes. Transfer to a cutting board and let stand 10 minutes. Cut into thin slices.

4. Heat remaining 2 tablespoons peanut oil in skillet over medium heat. Add mushrooms, bell peppers and snow peas; stir-fry until crisp-tender, 3 to 4 minutes.

5. Toss noodles with reserved oil mixture. Add steak and vegetables; toss to mix. Serve warm or at room temperature, sprinkled with cashews.

BACKYARD BASH FOR EIGHT

Spicy beef with noodles

Oriental cabbage

Sesame seed breadsticks

Fruit kebabs with gingered peach dipping sauce

Strawberry-topped ricotta cheesecake

Iced tea

STRAWBERRY-TOPPED RICOTTA CHEESECAKE WITH STRAWBERRY GLAZE

People get passionate about cheesecake. This ivory-colored beauty seems to satisfy everyone. It is luscious and creamy, unforgivably rich and easy to make. The strawberry topping is optional and open to many other seasonal ideas. Any type of berry, peaches or even a sweet cranberry relish can be used atop the cake.

Preparation time: 45 minutes
Cooking time: 1¹/₂ hours
Yield: One 9-inch cake

CRUST

1¹/₂ cups vanilla wafer or zwieback crumbs

¹/₄ cup (¹/₂ stick) unsalted butter, melted

FILLING

1¹/₄ cups sugar

¹/₄ cup (¹/₂ stick) unsalted butter, softened

3 large egg yolks

3 tablespoons flour

2 teaspoons pure vanilla extract

2¹/₂ pounds ricotta cheese

2 cups sour cream

Strawberry glaze, optional (recipe follows)

1. Heat oven to 325 degrees. Have ready a 9-inch springform pan.

2. For crust, mix crumbs and melted butter in small bowl. Press over bottom of springform pan. Bake until set, about 10 minutes. Cool on wire rack.

3. For filling, mix sugar, butter and egg yolks in large bowl of electric mixer until well mixed. Mix in flour and vanilla. Add ricotta and mix until smooth, 4 to 5 minutes. Mix in sour cream.

4. Pour into crust. Bake until filling is barely set in the center, 70 to 80 minutes. Cool to room temperature on wire rack. Refrigerate at least 4 hours before serving. Top with strawberry glaze if desired.

GLAZE

2 pints strawberries

³/₄ cup granulated sugar

¹/₄ cup cold water

1¹/₂ tablespoons cornstarch

1 teaspoon butter

1. Rinse and hull berries. Crush about 1 cup and place in a saucepan. Add sugar, water and cornstarch. Heat to a boil, then simmer, stirring constantly, for 2 minutes. Remove from heat; stir in butter. Cool to tepid.

2. Arrange remaining strawberries on top of the cheesecake. Spoon glaze over them. Chill until set.

CHICKEN WITH GARLIC, WINE AND TOASTED ITALIAN BREAD

Rustic and simple, this is Italian country food at its best. Serve the chicken at the table right from the pan so every last drop of the juices can be sopped up with the toasted bread.

Preparation time: 25 minutes
Cooking time: 40 minutes
Yield: 4 servings

---

1 broiler/fryer chicken, about
3 pounds, cut up

1/4 cup flour

1 tablespoon mixture of dried
thyme, oregano, basil

1/4 teaspoon dried sage leaves

Salt, freshly ground pepper to taste

1/2 cup olive oil

4 cloves garlic, minced

3/4 cup dry white wine

2 tablespoons minced Italian
parsley

12 or more slices Italian bread

1. Heat oven to 375 degrees. Rinse chicken; pat dry. Mix flour, herbs, salt and pepper in plastic food bag. Shake chicken in flour mixture to coat evenly. Shake off excess.

2. Heat oil in large, deep skillet over medium-high heat until hot. Add chicken pieces in single layer. Fry, turning occasionally, until light brown on all sides, about 15 minutes. Remove with tongs to paper towel-lined plate.

3. Pour off all but 2 tablespoons of the oil from the pan. Put chicken back into pan. Sprinkle with garlic. Pour wine over all. Bake, uncovered, until juices run clear, 20 to 25 minutes. Sprinkle with parsley.

4. Meanwhile, grill the bread, preferably over a fire or gas burner to achieve a rustic effect. Serve the bread with the chicken and pan juices.

ITALIAN SUPPER FOR FOUR

Chicken with garlic, wine and toasted Italian bread

Wonderful white beans with tomatoes and sage

Roasted pepper salad

Biscotti and fruit

Pino Grigio wine

WONDERFUL WHITE BEANS WITH TOMATOES AND SAGE

"Sweet Basil, Garlic, Tomatoes and Chives," a cookbook by Diana Shaw, celebrates the Italian penchant for creating sensational vegetable dishes from simple ingredients. This recipe turns tomatoes into a vibrant summer-into-fall dish that can be served as a salad or main course.

Preparation time: 20 minutes
Soaking time: Overnight
Cooking time: 50 minutes
Yield: 4 to 6 servings

---

1 cup dried white beans

3 cups lightly salted water

¼ cup extra-virgin olive oil

4 cloves garlic, crushed

2 pounds ripe tomatoes, seeded, chopped

Handful chopped fresh sage

Salt, freshly ground pepper to taste

1. Soak beans in plenty of cold water to cover in large bowl overnight. Drain.

2. Heat 3 cups lightly salted water to a boil. Add the beans and cook until soft but not mushy, about 50 minutes.

3. Meanwhile, heat the oil in a large skillet over medium heat. Add the garlic and cook until it starts to brown. Remove and discard the garlic. Add the tomatoes and sage to the oil. Cook, stirring often, until all the flavors are nicely blended, about 7 minutes.

4. Drain the beans and add to tomato mixture. Season with salt and pepper. Serve hot or at room temperature.

ROASTED PEPPER SALAD

Roasting bell peppers adds a smoky flavor to them and lends a marvelous texture, as this salad from columnist Abby Mandel illustrates so well. Roasting is a simple process, most easily done under the broiler. Another good option is to grill them.

Preparation time: 20 minutes
Marinating time: 1 to 4 hours
Cooking time: 10 minutes
Yield: 4 servings

---

3 large bell peppers, red and green

¹/₂ large Spanish onion, thinly sliced

¹/₂ cup Spanish olives

¹/₄ cup light-tasting olive oil

2 tablespoons red wine vinegar

1 small clove garlic, pressed through garlic press

Scant ¹/₂ teaspoon each: salt, sugar

1¹/₂ teaspoons water

1. Heat broiler. To roast peppers, stand them on board and cut sides off in four slabs. Arrange them, skin side up, on a baking sheet lined with aluminum foil. Broil, 6 inches from heat source, until skin is blackened. Wrap in foil. Slip off skin when they are cool enough to handle.

2. Place roasted pepper pieces on serving dish. Cover with onion slices, separated into rings. Scatter olives over. Put oil, vinegar, garlic, salt, sugar and water in blender; process to blend. Pour over salad. Cover with plastic wrap. Refrigerate at least 1 hour, no more than 4 hours. Serve chilled. Gently toss salad before serving.

AUTUMN ROOT VEGETABLE SOUP

All of the odd-looking members of the "root family" are apt candidates for the soup pot. Their earthy taste and soothing, rich texture are played to good advantage in this pale, golden-hued potage. In addition to those listed below, consider parsley root, rutabaga, turnips, sweet potatoes and winter squash.

Preparation time: 20 minutes
Cooking time: 40 minutes
Yield: 6 servings

$^{1}/_{4}$ cup ($^{1}/_{2}$ stick) **unsalted butter**

1 small **leek**, cleaned, thinly sliced

1 pound **celery root (celeriac)**, peeled, thinly sliced

$^{1}/_{4}$ pound **carrots**, peeled, thinly sliced

1 small **baking potato**, peeled, thinly sliced

1 rib **celery**, thinly sliced

4 cups **chicken stock or broth**

1 cup **whipping cream**

Salt, freshly ground pepper, cayenne pepper to taste

Freshly ground nutmeg to taste

$^{1}/_{4}$ cup **sour cream** for garnish

Shredded lime rind, for garnish, optional

1. Melt 2 tablespoons of the butter in a large saucepan. Add leek and cook gently until soft, about 5 minutes. Add celery root, carrots, potato and celery. Cook until carrots begin to soften, about 10 minutes.

2. Add stock; heat to boil. Cover; reduce heat and simmer until vegetables are thoroughly softened, about 20 minutes. Strain the solids from the liquid, reserving both. Puree the solids in a food processor or blender.

3. Combine the puree with the reserved liquid and return to the pan. Add remaining 2 tablespoons butter, whipping cream, salt, pepper, cayenne and nutmeg. Heat gently, until the soup is just below the boil. Remove from the heat and adjust the seasoning. Serve hot, drizzled with sour cream. Garnish with lime rind if using.

SPIRITED PARTY FOR SIX

Autumn root vegetable soup

Turkey burgers with spicy mustard

Santa Fe salad

Quick and easy fudge

Witches' brew punch

SANTA FE SALAD

Multicolored ingredients are combined with Southwestern flair in a salad that requires no cooking and that can be made ahead of time.

Preparation time: 20 minutes
Yield: 4 to 6 servings

DRESSING

1 jalapeno or serrano chili pepper, minced

6 tablespoons safflower oil

2 tablespoons sherry vinegar

1 teaspoon Dijon mustard

$1/2$ teaspoon ground cumin

$1/4$ teaspoon salt or more to taste

Freshly ground pepper

SALAD

1 medium each: sweet onion, zucchini

1 small red bell pepper

1 rib celery

1 can (16 ounces) black beans, rinsed, drained

$1/2$ cup sweet corn kernels

3 ounces Monterey Jack cheese, diced

1 cup loosely packed fresh cilantro leaves, chopped

1 ripe avocado

Red leaf lettuce for serving

1. For the dressing, combine all ingredients in a small bowl; mix well.

2. For the salad, dice the onion, zucchini, red pepper and celery into pieces that are roughly the size of the beans and corn. Combine in a large bowl with the beans, corn, cheese and cilantro. Just before serving, peel and dice the avocado and add to the salad along with the dressing. Mix gently and adjust the seasoning. Serve on lettuce leaves.

QUICK AND EASY FUDGE

Perhaps fudge isn't always so fussy and demanding after all. This luscious recipe, based on marshmallow creme, first appeared when the product did, in 1959. It's still enjoyed by kids of all ages.

Preparation time: 10 minutes
Cooking time: 7 minutes
Yield: About 2 dozen pieces

---

2 cups pecan or walnut halves

$2/3$ cup evaporated milk

1 jar (7 ounces) marshmallow creme

$1/4$ cup ($1/2$ stick) unsalted butter

$1^1/2$ cups sugar

$1/4$ teaspoon salt

1 package (12 ounces) semisweet or milk chocolate chips

1 teaspoon pure vanilla extract

1. Heat oven to 350 degrees. Have ready a 9-inch-square baking pan lined with aluminum foil.

2. Spread nuts on a baking sheet. Bake until lightly toasted and aromatic, 8 to 10 minutes. Watch carefully so they do not burn. Immediately remove to a plate to cool. Set $1/2$ cup aside for the top.

3. Put milk into a medium-size heavy-bottomed saucepan. Add marshmallow creme, butter, sugar and salt. Cook over medium-low heat, stirring constantly, until mixture comes to a boil. Reduce heat to low. Immediately start timing for 5 minutes, stirring constantly. Remove pan from heat; add chocolate chips; whisk until melted and smooth. Stir in vanilla and $1^1/2$ cups nuts. Quickly pour into the prepared pan. Smooth the top and arrange the $1/2$ cup nuts over the top.

4. Let stand until cool. Refrigerate until firm. Turn fudge out of pan; peel off foil. Cut into squares.

Note: For rocky road fudge, add 2 cups miniature marshmallows after adding nuts. For peanut butter fudge, use 1 package (10 ounces) peanut butter chips in place of chocolate chips and peanuts instead of walnuts. For white fudge, use 1 package (12 ounces) vanilla milk chips in place of chocolate chips.

SPICED CREAM OF SQUASH SOUP WITH CROUTONS

Small hollowed-out squash shells make whimsical tureens for a festive holiday table. Inside, they harbor a rich and soothing pureed soup, enlivened with the snap of a tart apple. The soup can be made several days in advance, although it should be gently reheated before the squash boats are filled.

Preparation time: 50 minutes
Cooking time: 1 hour
Yield: 8 servings

---

8 small acorn squash

2 tablespoons butter or margarine

2 medium leeks, white part only, chopped

1 medium carrot, chopped

1 clove garlic, minced

6 cups chicken stock or broth

1 medium apple, peeled, cored, chopped

1 bay leaf

$^1\!/_2$ teaspoon curry powder

$^1\!/_4$ teaspoon each, ground: nutmeg, white pepper, ginger

Salt, cayenne to taste

1 cup half-and-half or milk

Seasoned croutons

Shredded Gruyere or Swiss cheese

Chopped fresh cilantro, optional

1. Cut off top of each squash. Cut a thin slice off the bottom of each so squash sits level. Scoop out and discard seeds. Use a melon baller or grapefruit spoon to remove squash flesh, leaving a $^1\!/_2$-inch-thick shell. Reserve shells and flesh separately.

2. Heat butter in large saucepan. Add leeks, carrot and garlic; cook and stir until soft, about 5 minutes. Stir in squash flesh, chicken stock, apple and seasonings. Heat to boil; reduce heat. Simmer, uncovered, stirring often, until squash is very tender, 30 to 45 minutes.

3. Remove bay leaf. Puree soup in blender or food processor. Return soup to saucepan. Stir in half-and-half. Taste and adjust seasonings.

4. Ladle hot soup into reserved squash shells and serve. Or, if you like, heat broiler. Top each serving with a few croutons. Sprinkle with a few pieces of shredded cheese. Broil to lightly brown cheese and edge of squash shells. Sprinkle with cilantro. Serve immediately.

FEAST FOR EIGHT

Relish tray with vegetable dip

Spiced cream of squash soup with croutons

Roast turkey with pan gravy and apple-hazelnut stuffing

Brussels sprouts, carrots and parsnips with lemon chive vinaigrette

Mashed potatoes with chives

Sweet potatoes with maple syrup

Cranberry chutney or sauce

Pumpkin spice cake

Brandied pecan pie with whipped cream

Wine, sparkling cider

Coffee

ROAST TURKEY WITH PAN GRAVY AND APPLE-HAZELNUT STUFFING

The dogma that families make the same turkey stuffing every year appears to be mythic. At the Food Guide, *we get countless pre-Thanksgiving requests for new ideas to fill the big bird. This one, from food columnist William Rice, is different enough to answer the call but familiar enough to carry on tradition.*

Preparation time: 45 minutes
Cooking time: 3$\frac{1}{2}$ hours
Yield: 8 to 10 servings

---

8 to 12 cups cubed high-quality white bread

8 tablespoons unsalted butter

4 tart apples, cored, coarsely chopped

4 cups chopped celery, with some leaves

3 cups chopped onions

$\frac{1}{2}$ cup chopped fresh sage leaves

1 cup chicken or turkey broth

2 cups hazelnuts, toasted, skinned

Salt, freshly ground pepper to taste

1 turkey, about 14 pounds

Melted butter for basting

TURKEY PAN GRAVY

3 cups defatted pan drippings or turkey broth

3 tablespoons cornstarch

1 tablespoon dry red wine, optional

1. Heat oven to 250 degrees. Spread bread cubes on a baking sheet. Bake until bread is dry and crisp but not browned, 10 to 20 minutes.

2. Melt 4 tablespoons of the butter in a skillet over low heat. Add chopped apples to the pan; cook and stir over medium heat until tender, about 5 minutes. Spoon apples into a mixing bowl.

3. Add remaining 4 tablespoons butter to the pan. Add celery and onions; cook until softened, stirring occasionally. Add sage and cook briefly. Transfer contents of skillet to the mixing bowl along with bread cubes. Add broth and toss to mix. Stir in hazelnuts and salt and pepper to taste. Let cool.

4. Heat oven to 425 degrees. Rinse turkey under cold water; pat dry. Rub inside of turkey with salt. Spoon cooled stuffing loosely into cavity and neck end of bird to fill. Truss openings with kitchen string. Tuck wings underneath and tie legs together.

5. Put turkey onto oiled rack set in a roasting pan. Rub outside of turkey with melted butter. Roast, uncovered, at 425 degrees, for 30 minutes. Reduce oven temperature to 350 degrees and continue cooking until internal temperature is 170 degrees on a meat thermometer, 2$\frac{1}{2}$ to 3 hours. Baste the turkey occasionally with melted butter and any accumulated pan juices.

6. Transfer turkey to cutting board. Let stand, loosely tented with foil, 15 to 20 minutes before carving. Remove stuffing to a serving bowl.

7. Meanwhile, for gravy, remove fat from pan drippings. Measure drippings and add broth to make 3 cups. Pour all but $\frac{1}{2}$ cup of the drippings back into the roasting pan. Heat to a boil, scraping bottom of pan to dissolve any browned bits.

8. Mix the $\frac{1}{2}$ cup drippings with the cornstarch until smooth. Whisk cornstarch mixture into drippings in pan. Cook, whisking constantly, until smooth and thick. Add salt, pepper and wine if using.

BRUSSELS SPROUTS, CARROTS AND PARSNIPS WITH LEMON CHIVE VINAIGRETTE

To novice cooks, preparing turkey-and-all-the-trimmings seems to be an insurmountable task. To show readers how easy it really is to pull it off, we paired a Thanksgiving first-timer with Chicago cooking teacher Kristen James for our annual Thanksgiving article. James showed the novice the ropes and proved that preparing the holiday dinner is an easily managed series of steps. She also contributed this delicious recipe.

Preparation time: 25 minutes
Cooking time: 10 minutes
Yield: 8 to 10 servings

$^{1}/_{2}$ **cup each: extra-virgin olive oil, fresh lemon juice**

2 tablespoons honey

1 tablespoon mayonnaise

3 tablespoons minced fresh chives

$^{1}/_{4}$ **teaspoon each: grated lemon rind, freshly ground pepper**

Salt to taste

2 pounds fresh Brussels sprouts

1 pound each: carrots, parsnips

1. For vinaigrette, put olive oil, lemon juice, honey, mayonnaise, chives, lemon rind, pepper and salt into jar with tight-fitting lid. Shake well. Dressing can be made up to 3 days in advance and refrigerated.

2. Trim off any yellow outer leaves and the stem ends from Brussels sprouts. With a paring knife, cut a small X into the stem end. Peel carrots and parsnips. Cut lengthwise in half if large. Cut each crosswise into thirds.

3. Heat 2 large pots of water to boil. Cook Brussels sprouts in one pot until bright green and crisp-tender, 6 to 8 minutes. Cook carrots and parsnips in the other pot until crisp-tender, 6 to 8 minutes. Drain vegetables. (Rinse under cold water if making in advance. Drop into boiling water to reheat before serving.)

4. Toss hot vegetables together with vinaigrette. Serve immediately.

PUMPKIN SPICE CAKE

Even staunch traditionalists won't mind trading pumpkin pie for this buttery-rich beauty of a cake. The warm, autumnal taste is much the same but comes to the table in a different form. Abby Mandel featured it in her Weekend Cook column.

Preparation time: 30 minutes
Cooking time: 55 minutes
Yield: One Bundt cake

CAKE

2 cups cake flour

1 tablespoon baking powder

2 teaspoons cinnamon

1 teaspoon ground allspice

$^1/_2$ teaspoon each: baking soda, salt

1$^1/_3$ cups granulated sugar

$^3/_4$ cup (1$^1/_2$ sticks) unsalted butter or margarine, softened

3 large eggs, separated

1$^1/_4$ cups canned solid-pack pumpkin

3 tablespoons each: bourbon, buttermilk

SPICED SUGAR

2 teaspoons confectioner's sugar

$^1/_4$ teaspooon each: ground allspice, cinnamon

1. Put rack in center of oven. Heat oven to 350 degrees. Generously grease a large (12- to 14-cup capacity) Bundt pan. Lightly coat with flour, tapping out excess.

2. For cake, sift together flour, baking powder, cinnamon, allspice, baking soda and salt. Set aside.

3. Beat sugar, butter and egg yolks in large bowl of electric mixer until light and fluffy. Add pumpkin, bourbon and buttermilk. Mix until smooth, scraping down sides. Add flour mixture and mix until combined.

4. Beat egg whites in small bowl of electric mixer until they hold soft peaks and are still moist. Stir $^1/_4$ of egg whites into batter to lighten it. Fold in remaining whites. Transfer batter to prepared pan. Tap pan on counter several times to settle batter. Use knife to cut through batter to remove remaining air bubbles.

5. Bake until lightly browned and toothpick inserted in center comes out clean, about 55 minutes. Let cool in pan 5 minutes, then gently invert onto cooling rack.

6. To serve, combine confectioners' sugar and spices. Shake mixture through a fine wire-mesh sieve over surface of cake. Serve cake warm with caramel sauce if desired.

Note: Cake can be made a day ahead and kept at room temperature, covered airtight. It also can be frozen as long as 3 months, wrapped airtight. Reheat in 250-degree oven just to warm through, about 20 minutes.

BRANDIED PECAN PIE WITH WHIPPED CREAM

A generous splash of brandy and plenty of pecans puts this custardy nut-topped pie in a league of its own.

Preparation time: 40 minutes
Baking time: 40 to 50 minutes
Yield: One 9-inch pie

---

1 pie shell, 9-inch

3 large eggs

$1/2$ cup each: packed light brown sugar, whipping cream

$1/3$ cup dark corn syrup

2 tablespoons melted unsalted butter

$1/4$ teaspoon salt

2 tablespoons brandy, optional

1 teaspoon pure vanilla extract

$1^1/2$ cups pecan halves

Whipped cream for serving, optional

1. Heat oven to 375 degrees. Have pie shell ready.

2. Beat eggs, sugar, cream, corn syrup, butter and salt together in medium bowl. Stir in brandy, vanilla and pecans. Pour into pie shell.

3. Bake until filling is set and pie shell is golden brown, 40 to 50 minutes. Cool on wire rack before serving. Serve at room temperature with whipped cream.

POTATO AND ZUCCHINI LATKES WITH CHUNKY APPLESAUCE

There are many versions of crisp, fried potato pancakes and just as many opinions as to how they are best prepared. Many cooks applaud the day the food processor came along to help shred the potatoes, but there still are those who insist that a hand grater is the only way to get the proper texture. We opt for the food processor but offer a recipe that can be prepared either way. Traditionally, latkes are made with potatoes and onions, although zucchini or sweet potato can be added to the mix, too.

Preparation time: 20 minutes
Cooking time: 5 minutes per batch
Yield: About 15 pancakes

---

3 medium Idaho potatoes, 1$\frac{1}{2}$ pounds total, peeled

2 small onions

1 medium zucchini or sweet potato, optional

2 large eggs, lightly beaten

3 tablespoons matzo meal

2 teaspoons salt

Freshly ground pepper to taste

Vegetable oil for cooking

Chunky applesauce for serving

1. Grate the potatoes, onions and zucchini with the coarsest side of a 4-sided grater. Or, shred them with the shredding disk of a food processor. Using your hands, squeeze as much liquid from the gratings as possible. Transfer to a large bowl; add eggs, matzo meal, salt and pepper. Mix well.

2. Heat $\frac{1}{8}$ inch of oil in a non-stick griddle or large skillet over medium-high heat. Form pancakes, using about 3 tablespoons of the mixture for each one. Cook, turning once, until golden, about 5 minutes per batch. Serve with chunky applesauce.

FESTIVAL FOR EIGHT

Potato and zucchini latkes with chunky applesauce

Beef brisket with carrot and sweet potato tzimmes

Honey challah bread

Tossed salad with vinaigrette

Fried jelly doughnuts or
honey nut cake

Kosher wine

BEEF BRISKET WITH CARROT AND SWEET POTATO TZIMMES

Properly cooked, brisket is a tender and succulent cut of meat that adapts well to many different flavorings. Here, carrots, dried fruits, sweet potatoes and honey confer a festive note.

Preparation time: 25 minutes
Cooking time: 3 hours
Yield: 8 servings

---

1 beef brisket, preferably first-cut, about 3^1/$_2$ pounds

2 pounds carrots, peeled, sliced

4 cups beef broth

2^1/$_4$ cups water

1 teaspoon cracked black pepper

^{1}/$_4$ teaspoon dried thyme

3 tablespoons potato starch

1^1/$_2$ pounds medium sweet potatoes, peeled, thickly sliced

1 box (12 ounces) pitted prunes

^{1}/$_4$ cup honey

Salt, freshly ground pepper to taste

Chopped chives for garnish, optional

1. Heat oven to 350 degrees. Put brisket, carrots, broth, 2 cups of the water, pepper and thyme into 6-quart heavy-bottomed Dutch oven. Bake, covered, for 2 hours.

2. Mix remaining ^{1}/$_4$ cup water and potato starch in small bowl until dissolved; stir into pan juices. Add sweet potatoes, prunes and honey to pan. Continue baking, covered, until meat and potatoes are fork-tender, about 1 more hour. (If desired, let cool; refrigerate overnight. Skim off fat. Reheat over low heat.)

3. To serve, remove meat to cutting board; cut into very thin slices. Add salt and pepper to taste to carrot mixture in pan. Transfer to serving bowl. Garnish with chives.

HONEY CHALLAH BREAD

This golden egg braid is too good and too versatile to reserve only for the traditional Hanukkah meal. It makes a fine base for sandwiches and is especially good to use in bread pudding and for French toast. Though braiding the strands of dough is easily mastered, the dough also can be baked in loaf pans to simplify the task; baking time will be slightly shorter.

Preparation time: 30 minutes
Rising time: 2 to 3 hours
Cooking time: 40 minutes
Yield: 1 large loaf

---

2 packages active dry yeast

**1³/₄ cups warm water
(105 to 115 degrees)**

¹/₂ cup vegetable oil

¹/₄ cup honey

2 large eggs, beaten

1 tablespoon pure vanilla extract

³/₄ teaspoon salt

6 to 7 cups all-purpose flour, about

1 egg yolk, beaten

1. Dissolve yeast in ¹/₄ cup of the water in small bowl; let stand until bubbly.

2. Mix remaining 1¹/₂ cups water, oil and honey in large mixer bowl with dough hook or in food processor fitted with dough blade. Add 2 eggs, vanilla, salt and dissolved yeast; mix well. Gradually add flour to form a stiff dough. Knead, adding more flour as needed, until smooth and elastic, 5 to 10 minutes.

3. Put dough into large oiled bowl. Turn to oil top of dough. Cover loosely with damp towel. Let rise in warm place until doubled in bulk, 1 to 1¹/₂ hours.

4. Punch down dough. For one large double-braided loaf, cut dough into two portions, with one portion slightly larger than the other. Divide the larger portion into 3 pieces; roll each piece into a long rope. Braid the 3 ropes together. Repeat with the smaller portion of dough. Place the larger braid onto a well-greased baking sheet. Place smaller braid down center of larger braid. Brush with egg yolk.

5. Let rise, covered, until doubled in bulk, 1 to 1¹/₂ hours.

6. Heat oven to 350 degees. Bake until golden and bottom sounds hollow when tapped, about 40 minutes. Cool completely on wire rack.

CRACKLINGS AND GREENS CORN MUFFINS

Any self-respecting gumbo comes to the table along with a basketful of homemade corn muffins. These tender little gems are packed with lots of flavor, thanks to bits of bacon and collard greens.

Preparation time: 20 minutes
Cooking time: 25 minutes
Yield: 12 muffins

6 ounces thick-sliced slab bacon, about 6 strips

3/4 cup chopped greens, such as collard, mustard or turnip

1/4 cup chopped green onions

1 cup each: yellow cornmeal, all-purpose flour

3 tablespoons sugar

2 1/2 teaspoons baking powder

1/2 teaspoon crushed red pepper flakes

1/4 teaspoon salt

1 cup buttermilk

6 tablespoons unsalted butter, melted

1 large egg, beaten

1. Heat oven to 400 degrees. Generously grease muffin cups.

2. Chop bacon into small pieces. Cook in large skillet, stirring often, until crisp. Remove bacon with slotted spoon to paper towels. Cook chopped greens and green onions in bacon fat just until wilted, 2 to 3 minutes. Remove from heat.

3. Mix cornmeal, flour, sugar, baking powder, red pepper flakes and salt in large bowl. Stir in bacon and greens. Stir in buttermilk, melted butter and egg just until dry ingredients are moistened. Do not overmix.

4. Divide batter among greased muffin cups, filling each about 2/3 full. Bake until muffins are golden and have pulled away from sides of pan, 20 to 25 minutes. Cool on wire rack. Serve warm.

GUMBO PARTY
FOR SIX

Cracklings and greens corn muffins

Steamed rice

Romaine and black-eyed pea salad
with mustard vinaigrette

Shrimp and crab gumbo

Peach poundcake or ice cream

Assorted beers

Chicory coffee

SHRIMP AND CRAB GUMBO

Kwanzaa, an African-American holiday which runs from December 26 through January 1, is a time for reflection, affirmation and spiritual renewal. In addition to lighting a candle a day throughout the seven-day holiday, an important part of the Kwanzaa celebration is sharing a traditional African-American meal. A classic gumbo makes a fine centerpiece.

Preparation time: 25 minutes
Cooking time: 1 hour and
   15 minutes
Yield: 4 to 6 servings

$^1/_2$ cup each: peanut oil, flour

1 large onion, chopped

6 green onions, chopped

1 green bell pepper, diced

1 celery rib, diced

$^1/_4$ cup minced parsley

3 cloves garlic, minced

2 cans (14 ounces each) diced tomatoes

$^1/_4$ cup tomato paste

1 bay leaf

$^1/_4$ teaspoon each: salt, cayenne, dried thyme

Freshly ground pepper to taste

3 cups fish stock, clam juice or chicken broth

$^1/_2$ pound fresh okra, sliced, or 1 package (10 ounces) sliced frozen okra

1 pound large shrimp, peeled, deveined

12 to 16 crab claws, or 2 cooked blue crabs, quartered

Cooked white rice, hot red pepper sauce

1. Heat oil over medium heat in a large, heavy pot until hot. Stir in the flour; cook, stirring constantly, until mixture is a deep brown, about 7 minutes.

2. Stir in onion, green onions, green pepper, celery, parsley and garlic; cook and stir 5 minutes. Stir in tomatoes, tomato paste, bay leaf, salt, cayenne, thyme and pepper. Cook 5 minutes longer, stirring several times. Add the fish stock and heat to a simmer.

3. Meanwhile, heat a well-seasoned or nonstick large skillet over medium heat until hot. Add sliced okra; cook, turning once, until okra turns bright green, 3 to 4 minutes. Add okra to gumbo base. Cover; simmer, stirring often, about 1 hour. Taste and adjust seasonings.

4. Just before serving, add shrimp and crab to gumbo base. Cook until shrimp is opaque and crab is heated through, about 5 minutes. Serve immediately with rice and hot sauce.

SPICED CHAMPAGNE PUNCH

Oz Schoenstadt, proprietor of Oz, a very civilized watering hole on Chicago's North Side, dug into his extensive files and came up with this old recipe for holiday punch. It has an intriguing blend of flavors, with herbaceous and citrus tastes lurking just beneath the surface.

Preparation time: 10 minutes
Cooking time: 5 minutes
Standing time: 4 hours or overnight
Yield: 16 servings

1/2 cup each: sugar, water

1 tablespoon coriander seeds

1 cinnamon stick, about 2 inches

Rind of 1 lemon, removed with vegetable peeler

Rind of 1/2 orange, removed with vegetable peeler

1/2 cup kirsch

2 bottles champagne or sparkling wine, chilled

1 lemon, thinly sliced

1. Mix sugar and water in small saucepan. Heat to boil; simmer for 5 minutes.

2. Remove from heat and add coriander seeds, cinnamon stick, lemon and orange rinds. Let mixture stand at least 4 hours or overnight.

3. At serving time, strain spiced syrup over a block of ice into punch bowl. Add kirsch and stir well. Add champagne or sparkling wine and stir briefly. Float lemon slices in punch.

DINNER FOR EIGHT

Assorted cheeses and crackers

Spiced champagne punch

Beef tenderloin with crispy ginger and Madeira sauce

Oven roasted potatoes

Mashed rutabaga with black pepper

Steamed broccoli with lemon butter

Cranberry chutney

Santa Lucia buns

Deep apple-cinnamon bread

Berry cherry fruitcake

Wine, coffee

BEEF TENDERLOIN WITH CRISPY GINGER AND MADEIRA SAUCE

*Beef tenderloin is an unexpectedly easy cut of beef to cook. Here, it is gilded with
slivers of fried ginger and a rich wine sauce.*

Preparation time: 20 minutes
Cooking time: 45 minutes
Yield: 8 servings

**1 large piece fresh ginger, about
4 ounces, peeled**

Vegetable oil

**1 beef tenderloin, fully trimmed
and tied, about 4 pounds**

**1 tablespoon minced mixed fresh
herbs, such as thyme, rosemary,
cilantro, chives**

MADEIRA SAUCE

3 cups rich beef stock

$^1/_4$ cup Madeira

$^1/_4$ cup red currant jelly

1. Cut ginger into very fine julienne. Pat dry with paper towels.

2. Heat $^1/_2$-inch oil in a large skillet until hot but not smoking. Fry ginger, a small batch at a time, until crisp, about 1 minute. Drain on paper towels. Repeat to fry all ginger. Reserve crisps on a paper towel-lined baking sheet for up to several hours. Reserve oil.

3. Heat oven to 400 degrees. Brush tenderloin generously with reserved oil. Roll tenderloin in chopped herbs. Put tenderloin into a large shallow roasting pan. Roast until meat registers 130 degrees (rare) on an instant-read thermometer inserted into the thickest portion, about 35 to 45 minutes. Baste the meat with the oil and some of the pan juices once or twice during the cooking.

4. Remove tenderloin from oven and let rest on platter for 10 minutes before carving.

5. Meanwhile, for sauce, boil beef stock until reduced to 2 cups. Add madeira and jelly. Reduce by another $^1/_2$ cup to intensify flavors and thicken the sauce.

6. Remove any trussing strings from beef and carve into $^1/_2$- to 1-inch-thick slices. Serve on individual plates with a pile of ginger crisps and some of the Madeira sauce.

SANTA LUCIA BUNS

The Scandinavian tradition of serving these sweet, golden-toned buns on Christmas is said to bring good luck. According to Chicago-area caterer Jean True, it also brings a measure of sanity since they can be made well in advance and frozen.

Preparation time: 30 minutes
Rising time: 2½ hours
Baking time: 10 to 12 minutes
Yield: 16 buns

---

1 cup half-and-half or milk

¾ cup sugar

½ cup (1 stick) unsalted butter

1 teaspoon each: loosely packed saffron threads, salt

2 packages active dry yeast

¾ cup warm water (105 to 115 degrees)

5 to 6 cups unbleached all-purpose flour

3 large eggs

⅓ cup golden raisins

1 cup ground almonds

1. Heat half-and-half in small saucepan until hot. Remove from heat; add sugar, butter, saffron and salt. Mix until butter melts.

2. Stir yeast into the warm water in large mixing bowl; let stand until bubbly. Blend thoroughly. Add the saffron mixture. Stir in 2 cups of the flour; beat until smooth. Beat in 2 of the eggs, raisins and almonds. Stir in remaining flour to make a soft dough.

3. Turn the dough out onto a floured surface and knead until smooth and elastic, 5 to 8 minutes. Place in large buttered bowl and turn to coat. Cover with a towel and let rise in warm place until doubled in bulk, about 2 hours.

4. Punch down and place on lightly floured surface. Cut into 32 pieces. For the Santa Lucia buns, roll 2 pieces of dough into ½-inch-wide ropes. Make an X with the two ropes. Coil each of the four ends counterclockwise to resemble a snail. Repeat to make 16 buns. Cover the buns with a damp towel and let rise until doubled in bulk, about 30 minutes.

5. Heat oven to 375 degrees. Mix remaining egg with 2 teaspoons water and, before baking, brush the buns with the egg wash. Bake until golden brown, 10 to 12 minutes. Cool on wire racks.

DEEP APPLE-CINNAMON BREAD

A double dose of apples and a generous complement of sweet spices make this quick bread from columnist Abby Mandel a special treat. Exceptionally moist and rich, it stays fresh for several days.

Preparation time: 25 minutes
Cooking time: 55 to 60 minutes
Yield: 1 loaf

---

¹/₂ cup dried apple slices

³/₄ cup walnut halves

¹/₂ cup (1 stick) unsalted butter or margarine, softened

1 cup sugar

2 large eggs

1¹/₃ cups unsweetened applesauce

2 cups cake flour

1 teaspoon baking soda

¹/₂ teaspoon salt

2 teaspoons cinnamon

1. Put rack in center of oven; heat oven to 350 degrees. Generously grease a 9- by 5-inch aluminum loaf pan; dust lightly with flour. Set aside.

2. Mince apple slices and walnuts together in food processor fitted with metal blade; use on/off motion to control texture. Set aside in large mixing bowl.

3. Beat butter and sugar in food processor or electric mixer until light. Add eggs and beat until fluffy and smooth. Add applesauce and mix well. Transfer batter to apples and nuts in mixing bowl. Sift together flour, baking soda, salt and cinnamon. Add to mixing bowl. Use wooden spoon or rubber spatula to combine ingredients. Transfer to prepared pan.

4. Bake until loaf is dark brown and a toothpick inserted into center comes out clean, 55 to 60 minutes. Let rest on rack 10 minutes. Gently remove loaf from pan; cool completely on rack. Can be served immediately but best wrapped in foil and allowed to stand at room temperature overnight. Can be frozen up to 2 months, wrapped airtight (thaw in wrapping).

BERRY CHERRY FRUITCAKE

Despite all the bad jokes about fruitcake, the fruit-and-nut holiday cake has legions of fans who can't imagine Christmas without it. This one will appeal to those who profess not to like fruitcake. Generously laden with nuts and dried fruits and annointed with orange liqueur, it is a fine addition to the holiday dessert repertoire.

Preparation time: 30 minutes
Soaking time: 24 hours or more
Cooking time: 65 minutes
Yield: One 10-inch cake

CAKE

1 cup each: dried cranberries, dried cherries

¹/₂ cup orange-flavored liqueur, such as Grand Marnier

2¹/₄ cups pecan halves, coarsely chopped

1 cup plus 6 tablespoons (2³/₄ sticks) unsalted butter, softened

1 cup sugar

4 large eggs

1 cup sour cream

1 tablespoon each: finely chopped crystallized ginger, pure vanilla extract

3 cups all-purpose flour

1 teaspoon each: baking soda, baking powder

¹/₂ teaspoon salt

SYRUP

¹/₂ cup light corn syrup

¹/₄ cup (¹/₂ stick) unsalted butter

²/₃ cup orange-flavored liqueur

GARNISH, OPTIONAL

Pecan halves, candied cherries

Whipped cream for serving

1. Mix dried fruits and liqueur in bowl; cover tightly and let stand at room temperature at least 24 hours.

2. Heat oven to 325 degrees. Generously butter a 10-cup kugelhopf, Bundt pan or, for two smaller cakes, an 8-inch springform tube pan and a 8-by-4-inch loaf pan; dust the inside with flour, tapping out the excess. Spread the nuts on a baking sheet and bake until they are light brown and fragrant, 8 to 10 minutes. Set aside to cool.

3. Beat butter and sugar in large bowl of electric mixer at high speed until light and fluffy, about 2 minutes. Beat in eggs, one at a time, mixing well after each addition. Mix in sour cream, ginger and vanilla. In another bowl, stir together the flour, baking soda, baking powder and salt. On low speed, add flour mixture to butter mixture. Stop mixer and add nuts and fruit.

4. Transfer batter to prepared pan. Bake until toothpick inserted in the center comes out clean, about 55 to 65 minutes depending on pan size.

5. Just before cake is finished baking, make syrup: Heat corn syrup and butter to a boil. Remove from heat and add liqueur.

6. Remove cake from oven; pierce through it in several spots with a skewer. Slowly pour part of syrup over top, letting it seep through. Cool in pan on wire rack at least 2 hours. Invert onto wire rack and brush remaining syrup over surface.

7. Garnish with pecan halves and candied cherries. Serve small wedges of the cake with whipped cream.